3 Think of examples from your own surroundings.

D0707942

Labels

We write labels to name objects.
Labels should only be one or two words. They can be used to name things on drawings or diagrams. They don't need a full stop.

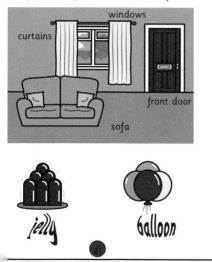

curtains

windows

front door

sofa

jelly

balloon

21

4 Try each different style of writing yourself.

LINCOLNSHIRE COUNTY COUNCIL	
03918129	
PETERS	£2.50
23-Aug-05	J372.6

Written by
Illustrated

Published
A
Penguin Books Ltd, 8
Penguin Books Australi
Penguin Books (NZ) Ltd, Cnr Airbourne an

1 3 5 7 9 10 8 6 4 2

© LADYBIRD BOOKS MMV

LADYBIRD and the device of a Ladybird are trademarks of Ladybird Books Ltd
All rights reserved. No part of this publication may be reproduced,
stored in a retrieval system, or transmitted in any form or by any means,
electronic, mechanical, photocopying, recording or otherwise,
without the prior consent of the copyright owner.

Printed in Italy

Writing for School

Letters	6
Writing a book review	8
Lists	10
Instructions	12
Writing an explanation	14
Observations	16
Questions	18
Captions	20
Labels	21
Posters	22
Signs	23
Writing a recount	24
Stories	26
Writing poetry	28
Try it yourself	30

Ladybird

Letters

There are many kinds of letters, such as letters asking for or giving information and letters to family and friends.

To write a letter you need to set it out properly. This is a thank you letter.

The name of the person you are writing to

Your address

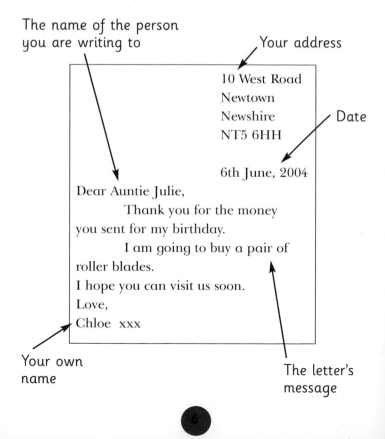

10 West Road
Newtown
Newshire
NT5 6HH

Date

6th June, 2004

Dear Auntie Julie,
        Thank you for the money you sent for my birthday.
        I am going to buy a pair of roller blades.
I hope you can visit us soon.
Love,
Chloe xxx

Your own name

The letter's message

To make sure your letter gets to the right person write the address clearly on the envelope.

Addie Parker,
8, Lower Street,
Springwell,
AA3 9TP

On postcards, the address goes next to your message.

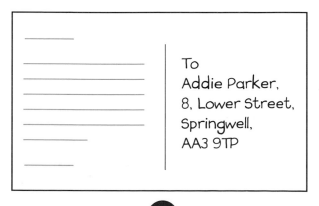

To
Addie Parker,
8, Lower Street,
Springwell,
AA3 9TP

Writing a book review

A book review is a chance for you to share your opinions about a book.

Jack and the beanstalk

The story:
Jack and the beanstalk is a great adventure story. Each time Jack went up the beanstalk I wanted to know what he was going to do next. It was exciting at the end when the giant started coming down the beanstalk.

Characters:
I didn't like the giant. He seemed mean and scary. I didn't like it when he said, 'Fe, Fi, Fo, Fum.'
I liked Jack because he was very clever and brave. He helped his mum by becoming very rich.

This is a very good book if you like adventure stories.

We write book reviews to tell others what is good or bad about a book we have read.

You need to include:

- What type of story it is: (adventure, detective, etc)
- Some things that happen in the story
- What you liked and didn't like
- Whether you think other people would enjoy the book, too.

Lists

When we write lists, the words don't have to be in a sentence. Usually we write the words going down the page.

My list of friends invited to the party

1 Johnny

2 Alfie

3 Darryl

4 Salim

5 Rebecca

6 Thea

We write to help us sort out things we have to do or things we need to get.

If there are a lot of items on the list, it is easier to put them into groups.

Lists remind us of things we need to do or get.

Ben's party to-do list

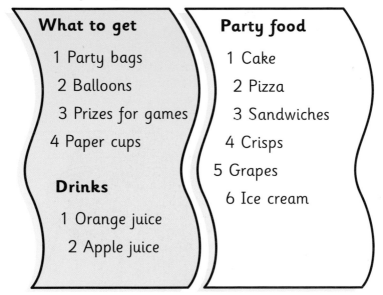

What to get

1 Party bags
2 Balloons
3 Prizes for games
4 Paper cups

Drinks

1 Orange juice
2 Apple juice

Party food

1 Cake
2 Pizza
3 Sandwiches
4 Crisps
5 Grapes
6 Ice cream

Some lists, such as address books or school registers, are written in **alphabetical order**. This is when the list starts with words beginning with **a**, and then moves on through the alphabet.

Useful vocabulary
list, to-do, alphabetical, contents, menu

Instructions

When you are writing instructions:

- write a list of what is needed
- write out what to do in simple steps.

How to make cheese on toast

What you need:

 A slice of toast

butter

 slices of cheese

What to do:

1 First, spread the butter on the toast.
2 Next, put the slices of cheese on the toast.
3 Then put the toast under the grill.
4 When the cheese is melted, take the toast out.
5 Finally, put the toast onto a plate.

We write instructions to show how something is done.

Sometimes instructions have drawings, or diagrams.

How to clean your teeth

 1 First, wet the toothbrush with cold water.

 2 Next, put the toothpaste on the toothbrush.

 3 Then, brush your teeth at the front and back.

 4 After that, spit out the toothpaste.

 5 Finally, rinse your teeth with clean water.

Useful vocabulary
first, next, then, after that, finally, diagram

Writing an explanation

It is best to start an explanation with a sentence which briefly sums up what you are writing about.

You can draw pictures or diagrams to go with your explanation writing.

A spider's web

1 A spider spins webs and catches small insects to eat.

2 First, the spider makes a silky thread from its body.

3 The spider swings on the thread to make a line between two things. This could be two leaves on a plant, or two gate posts.

4 The spider then spins its thread backwards and forwards until it makes a web.

5 When the web is finished, the spider sits in the middle and waits.

6 The web is sticky. Flies and small insects fly into it and get stuck. This is because the web is like a sticky net.

7 The spider climbs to the insects and eats them.

8 In the end, the web gets old and falls apart, so the spider spins another web somewhere else.

Useful vocabulary
because, then, when, so, in the end, finally

Observations

Here is an example of observational writing about ladybirds.

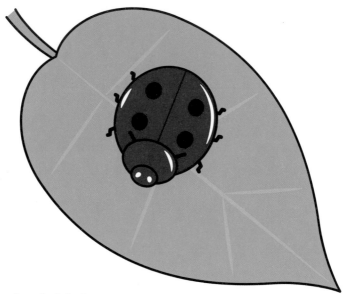

Ladybirds

A ladybird is a small beetle. It has two wings that sit on top of its body. The wings look like hard shells. They are bright red with two black spots, or sometimes more. It has six black legs. Its body is black and seems to be in three parts. There are tiny feelers, or antennae, on the head.

We use observational writing when we are describing the way something looks.

Before you start to write a description of something, you need to look at it closely. Use interesting and descriptive words in your writing.

Look at this picture of a butterfly.

You can write about:

- its shape
- its colours
- its size
- how it feels
- the different parts of its body
- what each part looks like.

Useful vocabulary
looks like, small, feels, big, size, same, colour

Questions

You can write questions to help you to find out information about other people.

1 What is your name?

2 How old are you?

3 What colour are your eyes?

4 Who are your friends?

5 Where do you live?

6 Do you have any brothers or sisters?

7 What is your favourite toy?

8 Do you have any pets?

Questions must always end with a question mark.

Questions often start with the words **who, which, when, where, why, how, is** and **do.**

We write questions to help us to find out information.

You could use some of the information from your questions to make a chart like this.

Our favourite toys

dolls   teddies   cars

1 How many children liked dolls?
2 How many children liked teddies?
3 What number of children liked cars?
4 What was the most popular toy?

Useful vocabulary
how, where, when, who, why, what, which, do, favourite

Captions

We write captions to give others simple information about something they are looking at.
Captions are usually one or two sentences. They all start with a capital letter.

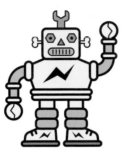

A model of a robot.

This is a diplodocus. It is 12 metres high and 40 metres long.

Labels

We write labels to name objects.
Labels should only be one or two words. They can be used to name things on drawings or diagrams. They don't need a full stop.

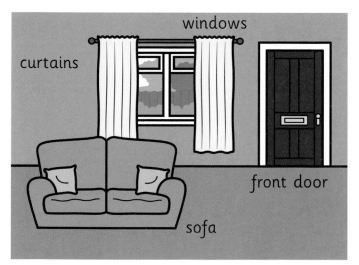

curtains

windows

front door

sofa

jelly

balloon

Posters

We create posters to tell others about important events or information.
To create a poster about an event, you need to write the date, the time and the place.

Make sure the letters are clear and large.

Who it is by

MARYLAND PRIMARY SCHOOL PRESENTS

ALADDIN

event

date

FRIDAY, 12TH MAY AT 2 O'CLOCK

time

in

place

THE SCHOOL HALL

TICKETS £3.00

price

Signs

We write signs to give out important information.
The words have to be simple and clear.
Colours and symbols help to explain meaning.
Warning signs are usually in capital letters.

Some signs are
all capital letters.

Some signs
use numbers.

Some signs use
more than one word.

Some signs have
both numbers and words.

Writing a recount

Recounts should be written in the past tense and they have to be written in the order that things really happened in.
The first sentence usually sets the scene.

This is a recount about a holiday trip.

My trip to the beach

On my holiday, I went to the beach.
First, I built a sandcastle with four towers.
Then I swam in the sea with my dad.
Next, I had my picnic lunch. I had cheese sandwiches. After that, I used my net in the rockpool. I found a starfish.
Finally, it was time to go home.
It was a great day.

We write recounts to talk about things that have already happened.

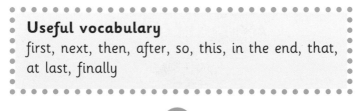

Useful vocabulary
first, next, then, after, so, this, in the end, that, at last, finally

Stories

Here are some different types of stories:
fairy tale, romance, adventure, spooky.

Before you write a story, you need to think of
a few things.

1 What is your story going to be about?
2 Where is your story going to be set?
3 What characters are going to be in
   your story?
4 How is your story going to start?
5 What will happen in your story?
6 How is your story going to end?

Before you write, make sure you know what kind of story you are writing.

To make your stories more interesting use descriptive words.

Fairy tales

cruel, evil, beautiful, misty, enchanted, handsome, magical, cunning, sly, honest, charming

Adventure stories

dangerous, exciting, heroic, greedy, vast, powerful, daring, magnificent

Ghost stories

creepy, eerie, weird, spooky, scary, spine-chilling, ghostly, gloomy

Useful vocabulary
Once upon a time, happily ever after, one day, suddenly, years later, there lived, wonderful

Writing poetry

Some poems are rhymes:

Peas porridge hot,
Peas porridge cold,
Peas porridge in the pot,
Nine days old.

Some poems can be short:

Jack, be nimble,
Jack, be quick,
Jack, jump over the candlestick.

There are many different kinds of poems. Usually each line of a poem starts with a capital letter.

You can write poems that describe a sound that you have heard.

Rain

Drip, drip, drop,
Drop, drop, drip,
Splish, splosh, splash,
Splash, splosh, splish.

This is the sound of the pouring rain,
As it beats against my window pane.

Drip, drip, drop,
Drop, drop, drip,
Splish, splash, splosh,
Splash, splosh, splish.

Useful vocabulary
poem, capital letter, rhyme, rhythm, sound

Write a story

You could start with one of these lines:

The day started just like any other, but then on the way to school I found...

On the corner of my street there is an old shop...

Write a poem

Think about words which are easy to rhyme and have a try at writing a poem.

Write a poem that doesn't rhyme.